IT

IS

TIME FOR WAR!

GOD HAS LICENSE TO KILL

Tella Olayeri
+2348023583168

Published By:

GOD'S LINK VENTURES

Email tellaolayeri@gmail.com

Website www.tellaolayeri.com

US Contact
Ruth Jack
14 Milewood Road
Verbank
N.Y.12585
U.S.A. +19176428989

DEDICATION

This book is dedicated to the **HOLY GHOST** for inspiring me to write this eye opener book.

APPRECIATION

My appreciation goes to my dedicated wife, **MRS NGOZI OLAYERI,** who typed the manuscript of this book and design the cover page.

My darling wife I say thank you. My appreciation equally goes to my lovely children, **MISS IBUKUN, DAVID, MICHAEL, COMFORT and MERCY.** They encouraged me day and night as I write this book. Hurray, after seven years of research, reading, listening to counsels and support of the Holy Spirit etc. the long awaited book, bad dream enemies use to rob blessing and the way out is out!

Respect and honor should be given to who is due. Favor comes from God and men as well. My calling (writing evangelism) met the timely support of a particular man of God, preacher, teacher, prophet and General Overseer. He awakes my inner man, gave me sound spiritual support and stood by me in fulfillment of my calling.

This book you are holding is a testimony of my claim. This book wouldn't have seen the light of the day, if not for the spiritual encouragement I gathered from my father in the Lord who served as spiritual mirror that brightens my hope to explore my calling.

I am talking of no any other person than the **General Overseer of *MOUNTAIN OF FIRE AND MIRACLES MINISTRIES WORLD WIDE*, DR. D. K. OLUKOYA.**

Once again, I say thank you sir. Your support has yielded yet another earth shaking book.

THANKS

Evangelist Tella Olayeri.

PREFACE

The Lord Almighty is the only one that has license to kill. This book reminds us, He is a killer! He kills when it is justified and nothing happens. He can kill in the night and in the day as well. He can kill young, infant, or old. God is Almighty, no one can question. The Bible makes us to understand this when we read the history of the flood, championed by Noah and his Ark. The people of Sodom did evil and were killed. Pharaoh was obstinate to God and paid dearly for it. After paying with the first born sons in Egypt at night, they paid more when his Chariot men died in the Red Sea. There are many incidences discussed in this book with accurate reasons we establish the fact that God is a killer.

This book gives account of how wasteful, wasters encroach and destroy lives and properties, career and callings of people. We must rise up to check their activities and silence them. It is not a fun fare for a destiny to be wasted. If not checked or prayed against, it can lead to generational curse or generational circle of poverty and ill-luck. Wasters of destiny are faceless and wicked. They destroy virtues of people or keep it in warehouse of darkness. Destiny waters can run family down as well. When a bread winner of a family is killed, the family is in disarray. This is more reason, you must rise and kill witchcraft powers that vow to kill you or kill your bread winner. When pillar of a house is brought down, the house shakes and fall. This is the situation when a bread winner dies in a house.

This book educates us how we can evade the vow of the wicked. It is a law in the kingdom of darkness when the wicked made vow or come together against a person in covenant. This book treats negative vow or the vow of the wicked. Vow of wickedness is a vow made by the enemy, and or, witchcraft agents like herbalist, office co-workers, unfriendly friend, evil neighbor, satanic family member, church member, opposite religion member etc., to do evil. Those who make such vow mean business. They mean to kill. They mean to bury destiny. They mean to cause poverty in a life. They mean to cause sorrow and tears in a life. They mean to naked there victims. They consult evil places to settle scores with you. They mean to harm you, if possible, to make you run mad. They do all possible within them to remove protection of God in a life. They can fire arrow of prayerlessness into a life, so that you won't equip yourself with prayer or with Word of God.

Whatever the situation, you have duty of personal cleansing to carry out. Witchcraft spirit does not necessarily mean you are a witch, but your action can be equated to it. Witches are noted to kill, to steal and destroy destiny, so are other spirits that are satanic. Witches and wizards, herbalists, marine spirits, occult spirits are witchcraft spirit.

But then, there are spirits planted in a life through witchcraft food or initiation, and or, as a result of peer group. Spirit of drunkenness is a witchcraft spirit because it is an ungodly spirit that operates in such life. Spirit of lust is either inherited from parent, from peer group or developed inside of you as a result gullible mind or worldliness. Whichever way, witchcraft spirit is behind it all.

No matter how prayerful you are, enemy will create time to go after you. They are called stubborn pursuers. Definitely they will come, but the Lord will make you overcome them all. God's support for you will not make you live in anguish.

This book is recommended for you. Pick it.

GOOD NEWS!!!

My audiobook is now available, to get one visit **acx.com** and search **"Tella Olayeri."**

Brethren, to be loaded and reloaded visit: amazon.com/author/tellaolayeri for a full spiritual sojourn for my books.

Thanks.

PREVIOUS PUBLICATIONS OF THE AUTHOR

1. 100% CONFESSIONS and PROPHECIES to Locate Helpers and helpers to locate you
2. 1000 Prayer Points for Children Breakthrough
3. 1010 (One Thousand and Ten) DREAMS and Interpretations
4. 2000 Dangerous Prayer for First Born
5. 365 DREAMS and INTERPRETATIONS
6. 430 Prayers to Cancel Bad Dreams and Overcome Witchcraft Powers part one (DREAMS AND YOU Book 1)
7. 430 Prayers to Claim Good Dreams and Overcome Witchcraft Powers part two (DREAMS AND YOU Book 2)
8. 630 Acidic Prayers: With Missile Prayer for Speedy Breakthrough, Healing and Deliverance
9. 650 DREAMS AND INTERPRETATIONS
10. 700 Prayers to Clear Unemployment Out of Your Way
11. 720 Missile Prayers that Silence Enemies: Prayers that Bring Peace and Rest
12. 740 Rocket Prayers that Break Satanic Embargo
13. 777 Deliverance Prayers for Healing and Breakthrough
14. 800 Deliverance Prayer for Middle Born: Daily Devotional for Teen and Adult

15. <u>800 Deliverance Prayer Points for First Born: Daily Devotional for Teen and Adult</u>

16. <u>800 Deliverance Prayer Points for Last Born: Daily Devotional for Teen and Adult</u>

17. <u>830 Prophecies for the Head: Deliverance Prayer Book for the Brain, Eye, Ear and Mouth</u>

18. <u>Acidic Prayer against Dream Killers</u>

19. <u>Anointing for Eleventh Hour Help: Hope and Help for Your Turbulent Times</u>

20. <u>Atomic Decree that Opens Great Doors</u>

21. <u>Atomic Prayers that Destroy Destiny Killers</u>

22. <u>Atomic Prayers that Destroy Witchcraft Powers and Silence Enemies</u>

23. <u>Biblical Prayer against Sickness and Diseases: Winning the Battle Against Diseases</u>

24. <u>Calling God to Silence Witchcraft Powers: Prayers That Rout Demons</u>

25. <u>Children Deliverance: Power of a Praying Parent</u>

26. <u>COMMAND the DAY: 365 Days of Prayer for Christian that Bring Calm & Peace</u>

27. <u>Command The Night 30 Days Spiritual Manual Prayer Book: A Devotional Prayer Book With 1,200 Violent Prayer Points For Healing Breakthrough and Divine Acceleration</u>

28. <u>Command the Night Against 100 types of Witchcraft Arrows: Powerful Prayers in the War Room</u>

See all at: amazon.com/author/tellaolayeri

Table of Contents

CHAPTER 1

GOD HAS LICENSE TO KILL

God has license to kill and he is a killer! Don't doubt me, I say, God has license to kill and he is a killer! Yes, my God is a killer. You must take after God to kill! You must do what God did and is still doing to this day. Yes brethren, you are right to look straight to my eyes and ask; "Why are you so harsh, stubborn, senseless, arrogant, stupid and unbiblical to say the LORD Almighty, the King of kings, Yahweh is a killer?" Yes you may say I step over my boundary, you are correct to an extent, but until you are through with this chapter. The fact is, I am none of the above remark. I want you to know that when God rise to fight a just cause, he kills, at times in thousands. Let me tell you, God prepared and use the first atomic bomb in the Bible! Are you alright with my analysis? Let's read on.

Before we go on, I advise, *"Put on the full armor of God so that you can take your stand against the devil's scheme" Ephesians 6:11-12.* You must be fortified. You must be fearless. You must have faith. You must not indulge in sin. You must evade pride. You must love your neighbor. Yes, love your neighbor. When Jesus was asked, which the greatest commandment is, Jesus replied: *"Love the Lord your God with all your heart and with all your soul and with all your mind. This is the first and greatest commandment. And the second is like it: 'Love your neighbor as yourself'. All the law and the prophets hang on these two commandments" Mathew 22:37-40.*

God will never send you on errand to go and kill your perceived enemy. The person you pick as enemy may be one that God raised for a particular mission or purpose in your life. God allowed him to cross your line so that you may wake to fulfill your vision, to train you and acquire wisdom or teach you lesson. If you dare go after him, and kill him, you will be charged for murder and end up in jail or hanged.

In the Old Testament period, you will read how God killed severally at different times as circumstances warrant. Let's have a look at a number of them, before we go deep into how you will prepare for war and kill. Also, we shall know what to kill, and who shouldn't be killed. You can't kill as an individual, it is the primary function of court of law to pronounce death sentence on a person after careful consideration of circumstances that surround the situation. What are the circumstances that surround such situation? Which circumstances warrant us to kill? At this junction let's see why we say, God is a killer and has license to kill.

God was a killer in the time of Noah. Despite the preaching, prophecy, and warning of Noah, men went about doing what they love doing best. They scorn and mock Noah. When it was time to carry out his action, God arise and sent heavy rain that flooded the earth, killing everyone, except the family of Noah and chosen animals. I pray, animal will not replace you, in the name of Jesus.

In the case of Sodom and Gomorrah, we can see how furious God was to them. They committed abomination, men slept with men. The horrible situation caught attention of God, only Lot's family was saved, by the angel. They were led outside the city and fire breakout in Sodom consuming them all.

When we look at what God did in Egypt, we can safely call God a **"Double killer"**! Pharaoh was obstinate and stubborn against simple command of "Let my people go" Moses was sent to Pharaoh with the simple instruction to let the children of Israel go and worship the Lord in the wilderness. He told Pharaoh, but Pharaoh refused. It was not until God strike the entire firstborn son in Egypt with death, leaving children of Israel out of it,

Pharaoh obliged. God killed the entire first born of Egypt. **Round one**

Next was when Pharaoh out of fear and misery, let the children of Israel go, he changed his mind. He ordered all his able bodied chariot men to go after them and bring them back. They failed in the mission. They all drown and perished in the Red Sea. **Round two. Yes, God is a "Double killer!"**

The unimaginable happened when Korah, Dathan and Abiram ganged up against Moses. They challenged his superiority over the Israelites. Moses took the matter to God, and God answered him by fire. In any situation you meet yourself and you are challenged, call unto God and He will answer you by fire, in the name of Jesus. Amen. That day, something strange happened, the first earthquake open wide it's mouth and swallowed Moses enemies, including the families of the rebels. They all die. My prophecy unto you today is those who gang up against you shall scatter, in the name of Jesus.

Brethren, I advise you don't rebel against God with your mouth. Don't reduce or be-little yourself. God is not God of people that lost hope. Our God is a hope builder, have faith. When the twelve were sent by Moses, to go and spy out the Promised Land, they came back with discouraged information. They said, the land is good, but the people that inhabit it were like giants. Among the twelve, only Joshua and Caleb, have different opinion. They encouraged the congregation to have hope in God who will fight the battle for them. God was angry with the evil report and pronounced death to the ten and adults among them. He said they will surely die and not step into the Promised Land. Not quite long, they all die in battle as they march on and were never part of the people that occupy the Promised Land. Can you now see that God is a killer?

Let's look at how God killed with Atomic Bomb in the bible. When Joshua and the Israelites settled down in a camp of Gilgal, beside the Gibeonites, five kings declared war against the Gibeonites. When the Gibeonites saw they couldn't match the enemy they sent message to Joshua for help. Joshua rise to the situation and with the support of God, Joshua rout out the five kings that unite to fight Gibeonites. When they saw the battle was hot, they tried to escape, but God sent hailstones down on them from the sky and they died. This is the first heavenly bomb thrown down from the sky to destroy enemies of Israel. Today, God shall silence every power that gang up to fight you. Amen.

God did not only kill in the Old Testament, He did it in the New Testament as well. When Herod equated himself with God, he wore his royal robes, sat on the throne and delivered a public address to the people. *They shouted, "This is the voice of a god, not of a man" Acts 12:22.* Immediately worm ate him up.

Also, when Ananias and Sapphira sold their property and kept some behind for personal use, Holy Spirit struck them one after the other, as a result of unfaithfulness. God doesn't joke with unfaithfulness, it is counted as rebellion, and rebellion is witchcraft.

Brethren, arise in full force now, don't look back, be at alert, let your courage increase, be brutal with powers contending with your glory. Pray fire prayer and bring them down. If God kills and you are a child of God you have license to kill witchcraft powers that rise up against you. The time is now, let's pray.

PRAYER POINTS

1. I thank you Lord for your protection and love for me, in the name of Jesus

2. I thank you Lord for disgracing powers behind my challenges in the name of Jesus.

3. I thank you Lord, for giving me hope, in the name of Jesus.

4. Spirit that sin, my life is not for you, get out of my life, in the name of Jesus.

5. Lord Jesus, have mercy upon me, in the name of Jesus.

6. I seek forgiveness, O Lord, forgive me, in the name of Jesus.

7. I cover myself with blood of Jesus.

8. I drink blood of Jesus to purge me of evil deposit in the name of Jesus.

9. Blood of Jesus, be a mark in my body against satanic invasion, in the name of Jesus.

10. Holy Spirit Divine, fill my heart in the name of Jesus.

11. Holy Spirit, prepare me for war and let me win, in the name of Jesus.

12. Holy Ghost Fire, consume powers that gathered to disgrace me, in the name of Jesus.

13. O Lord, disgrace every stubborn pursuer that rise against me, in the name of Jesus.

14. O Lord, kill and bury every power that vow to kill me, in the name of Jesus.

15. O Lord, do for me what you did in the past, kill powers that vow I will not reach my Promised Land, in the name of Jesus.

16. O Lord, equip me with your full armour to stand against the devil's scheme, in the name of Jesus.

17. O Lord, fortify me with fire in my mouth, in the name of Jesus.

18. Powers controlling the dark world, assign to control me, expire in the name of Jesus.

19. Every dark authority molesting me in my sleep, die, in the name of Jesus.

20. Rulers of darkness assigned to trouble my destiny, my life is not your candidate, expire, in the name of Jesus.

21. Powers in flesh and blood, troubling me, be disgraced in the name of Jesus.

22. Every arrogant and senseless spirit planted in my life, come out of me and expire, in the name of Jesus.

23. Every evil remark against me, be nullified in the name of Jesus.

24. Powers that rise up in order to attack me be put to shame in the name of Jesus.

25. Any power that wants to contend with God your obituary is today, expire, in the name of Jesus.

26. Every terror at night shall swallow my enemies in the order of death of Egyptian first born, in the name of Jesus.

27. I shall not be cut down by arrows that fly by night in the name of Jesus.

28. I shall not be cut down by arrows that fly by day, in the name of Jesus.

29. Powers that look straight to my eyes, and ask, "Why do I serve my God" go blind in the name of Jesus.

30. O Lord, incubate me with fearless spirit of God to face and win my enemies, in the name of Jesus.

31. Every evil command pronounced against my destiny, backfire in the name of Jesus.

32. Evil spirit that direct me to kill my neighbor, die and rise no more, in the name of Jesus.

33. Heavenly court, pronounce death upon enemies of my soul, in the name of Jesus.

34. Every warning in the dream assign to reshape my life, I connect my life to you, in the name of Jesus.

35. Horrible situation that demote life, hunting me, scatter, in the name of Jesus.

36. O Lord, don't be furious against my family in the name of Jesus.

37. O Lord, apply the power of double killer, against my enemy in the order of Egypt, left and right, in the name of Jesus.

38. O Lord, use the power of double killer against my enemy, in the order of Egypt, front and back, in the name of Jesus.

39. O Lord, use the power of double killer against my enemy, in the order of Egypt, above and below, in the name of Jesus.

40. Every evil mission against my destiny, scatter, in the name of Jesus.

41. O Lord, destroy every stubborn pursuer that refuse to let me go, in the name of Jesus.

42. O Lord, harden the heart of my enemy until they perish in the name of Jesus.

43. Stubborn Pharaoh in the spirit, leave me alone and die, in the name of Jesus.

44. Every Pharaoh against me, bow before my Moses, in the name of Jesus.

45. Every abomination assigned to swallow my destiny, scatter in the name of Jesus.

46. Powers that vow my God will not favor me shall die, in the name of Jesus.

47. Spirit of pride in my life, come out of me in the name of Jesus.

48. Every evil errand of darkness to suffocate my destiny scatter; in the name of Jesus.

49. Spirit of Sodomy shall not locate my family in the name of Jesus.

50. Where human beings are counted, animal will not replace me in the name of Jesus.

51. My family, live above sudden death in the name of Jesus.

52. Every trap set, to catch me, catch your owner, in the name of Jesus.

53. Flood of darkness shall not sweep me away in the name of Jesus.

54. Flood of darkness shall not sweep my family away in the name of Jesus.

55. Every mockery that block heavenly breakthrough, expire, in the name of Jesus.

56. Every prophecy spoken concerning my life, O Lord, open my eyes to see it, in the name of Jesus.

57. O Lord, have mercy on me don't harvest my soul before my time in the name of Jesus.

58. O Lord, multiply my faith, in the name of Jesus.

59. O Lord, give me spirit to love my neighbor, in the name of Jesus.

60. O Lord, empower me to love my God with all my heart in the name of Jesus.

61. Every step I take to fulfill my dream in life, appear in the name of Jesus.

62. Heavenly wisdom, my life is available enter in the name of Jesus.

63. Helpers of my destiny appear by fire and help me in the name of Jesus.

64. A thousand may fall at my side, they will not near me, in the name of Jesus.

65. Ten thousands may fall at my right side; I will only observe them with my eyes, in the name of Jesus.

66. Powers that against me to worship my God, expire in the name of Jesus.

67.O Lord, silence every power that captivate my destiny in the name of Jesus.

68.O Lord, strike enemy that vow "I shall not let you go" with paralysis, in the name of Jesus.

69.Satanic wilderness assigned to consume me, catch fire and burn to ashes, in the name of Jesus.

70.O Lord, let your instruction sink into my head, in the name of Jesus.

71.Arrow of untimely death, fired to destroy me, backfire to the sender, in the name of Jesus.

72.O Lord, let my enemy that changed mind to kill me, expire and rise no more in the name of Jesus.

73.Soldiers of darkness on chariot after my life, die in the name of Jesus.

74.Powers that pursue me in the spirit to delay my breakthrough, expire in the Red Sea in the name of Jesus.

75.Every arrow of backwardness fired against me, backfire in the name of Jesus.

76.O Lord, let the enemy of my destiny, meet failure upon failure, in the name of Jesus.

77.Every mission of darkness to make me cry, scatter in the name of Jesus.

78.O Lord, let fear and misery make my enemy to make everlasting mistake of shame and disgrace, in the name of Jesus.

79.Every gang up against me scatter in the name of Jesus.

80.O Lord, let wicked decision of evil gang up against me, scatter in the name of Jesus.

81.O Lord, disgrace my junior that wants to unseat me in office, in the name of Jesus.

82.Power assign to pull down my star, my destiny is not your candidate, expire in the name of Jesus.

83.O Lord, let something strange that will make my enemy surrender forever happen today, in the name of Jesus.

84.Every challenge of enemy against me scatter, in the name of Jesus.

85. O Lord, I table my matter before you, destroy enemy assign to destroy me, in the name of Jesus.

86. Earthquake of God, shake the foundation of where my enemies reside, in the name of Jesus.

87. Earthquake of God, consume stubborn pursuers that vow to kill me in the name of Jesus.

88. Thou earth, open and swallow powers that gang up against me in the name of Jesus.

89. Heavenly key of hope, I possess you in the name of Jesus.

90. Every hopeless situation, expire, in the name of Jesus.

91. Messenger of failure advancing towards me, turn back, in the name of Jesus.

92. Every giant on my way to success, be consumed by fire of God, in the name of Jesus.

93. O Lord, build my hope to occupy mountain top in the name of Jesus.

94. Dark information box against my soul, catch fire and burn to ashes in the name of Jesus.

95. I shall not be like grasshopper anywhere I go, in the name of Jesus.

96. I will occupy my Promised Land, in the name of Jesus.

97. O Lord, turn the giants in my life to dwarf in the name of Jesus.

98. O Lord, empower me to confront every battle that confronts me in the name of Jesus.

99. I shall not die in the battle of life in the name of Jesus.

100. Every evil report written against me catch fire and roast to ashes in the name of Jesus.

101. O Lord, scatter the language and understanding of my enemy in the name of Jesus.

102. O God arise, throw hailstones from heaven and kill powers that surround me, in the name of Jesus.

103. O God arise, throw hailstones from heaven and kill powers that flee as I pray in the name of Jesus.

104. O Lord, multiply my wealth and let your joy fill my heart in the name of Jesus.

105. O Lord, silence powers assign to silence me in the name of Jesus.

106. I shall not be fed by enemy in the name of Jesus.

107. I shall witness ship of wealth and investment, my lamentation is over in the name of Jesus.

108. Powers that try to escape in this prayer battle shall fall by the sword of angels of God, and shall rise no more in the name of Jesus.

109. Heavenly bomb, kill powers that never stop to attack me in my dream, in the name of Jesus I pray. Amen.

CHAPTER 2

PRAYING AGAINST DESTINY WASTERS

Destiny wasters are destiny killers. If your destiny is not killed or robbed, you will achieve good things of life. Enemies that rob destiny knew the business they are into. They are emptier of hope, they make you hopeless. They rob you or scatter your destiny so that you may be a perpetual beggar, a moron, a thief in the society, a drug addict, a robber, a thug, a penury person, a dejected man or woman, a person of sorrow and a man or woman in the valley.

It is not a fun fare for a destiny to be wasted. If not checked or prayed against, it can lead to generational curse or generational circle of poverty and ill-luck. Wasters of destiny are faceless and wicked. They destroy virtues of people or keep it in warehouse of darkness. Destiny wasters can run a family down. When a bread winner of a family is killed, the family is in disarray. This is why you must rise and kill witchcraft powers that vow to kill you or kill your bread winner. When pillar of a house is brought down, the house shakes and fall. This is the situation when a bread winner dies in a house.

Your destiny is your life. When life is sniffed out of you, the grave is the next destination. I pray, your body shall not know grave at your prime age. Wasters of destiny are suckers of destiny. They will suck you like orange and throw you away or into dustbin. Life in the dustbin is a wasted life. Witchcraft powers are dare devil. They hunt life until it's wasted. They use every means available to them, to distract you from pursuing your dream and direct your steps to ruinous path that demote life.

Brethren, do you know you are a peculiar person? Yes, you are peculiar; no two persons are like you on earth. You are yourself and so is your talent. But, once your talent is altered, your destiny is wounded and captivated. To avoid this, you must pray and kill wasters of destiny assigned to kill your destiny. This is the reason you must be a killer in the spirit, to kill famine, poverty, sorrow, ill-luck, rejection, shame, backwardness, stagnancy, bareness, career killers and many more.

Be a soldier of Christ that knows his onions, that takes the bull by the horn, that doesn't catch fish by the tail, but violent, fearless and calculative in the spirit. You must make total declaration against Satan and his agents. Declare war now and fight the battle. Brethren, it is time to kill wicked powers, challenges, wicked spirits and every manner of powers of darkness that vow to destroy you. Our God is a killer of evil; take a clue from Him, eliminate witchcraft powers and be set free.

PRAYER POINTS

1. I thank my God for his love ad mercy upon me and my family in the name of Jesus.

2. I thank you Lord for your protection over me in the name of Jesus.

3. I thank my God who delivers me from attack of destiny killers in the name of Jesus.

4. Heavenly forgiveness; locate my life in the name of Jesus.

5. Lord Jesus, don't look at my unrighteousness, I surrender my life to you help me and forgive me by your power.

6. O Lord, let your forgiveness upon me be total, in the name of Jesus.

7. My blood, receive heavenly strength, in the name of Jesus.

8. My blood, be immunized against witchcraft attack, in the name of Jesus.

9. Blood of Jesus, cover me from head to toe against destiny killers in the name of Jesus.

10. Holy Spirit, guide my steps to breakthrough, in the name of Jesus.

11. Holy Ghost Fire, consume powers troubling my soul in the name of Jesus.

12. Holy Spirit, arrest wasters assign against me and kill them, in the name of Jesus.

13. O Lord, silence every waster assign to waste my destiny, in the name of Jesus.

14. O Lord, equip me with weapons of war to kill and destroy destiny killers assign against me, in the name of Jesus.

15. Every initiation of my soul to hard drug, break in the name of Jesus.

16. Power calculating days and months to attack me, expire, in the name of Jesus.

17. Helpers that reject me in the past, m life is available, locate me, in the name of Jesus.

18. Emptier of hope assigned to empty my destiny, my life is not your candidate, receive arrow of God and die, in the name of Jesus.

19. Every arrow of hopelessness fired against me; backfire in the name of Jesus.

20. Every arrow of famine fired against me; backfire in the name of Jesus.

21. Every arrow of ill-luck fired against me; backfire to your sender in the name of Jesus.

22. Every arrow of rejection and shame fired against me, I am not your candidate, reverse back and consume your sender, in the name of Jesus.

23. Every arrow of stagnancy and backwardness fired to scatter my career, backfire in the name of Jesus.

24. Every arrow of bareness fired against my marriage, backfire and destroy your sender in the name of Jesus.

25. Every arrow of insanity fired against my health; backfire in the name of Jesus.

26. Every arrow of poverty fired against me, to empty my life, backfire in the name of Jesus.

27. Robbers of destiny after my life, I fire you, die, in the name of Jesus.

28. Spirit of thug enemy planted in my life to rob me of good things of life, come out of me by fire in the name of Jesus.

29. Sword of God, locate my hands to kill powers assign to kill me, in the name of Jesus.

30. Evil plantation growing in the garden of my life, wither and die, in the name of Jesus.

31. Spirit of penury in my life, come out of me by fire in the name of Jesus.

32. Every party held for my sake, scatter, in the name of Jesus.

33. I recover my virtues in the camp of the enemy in the name of Jesus.

34. Every generational curse affecting my destiny, break in the name of Jesus.

35. Every arrow fired against breadwinner in my family backfire in the name of Jesus.

36. Destiny killers assigned to run my family down, die in the name of Jesus.

37. Witchcraft power that vow to suck my blood, you are a failure, my blood is bitter, I fire you, die, in the name of Jesus.

38. My virtues in the warehouse of darkness, I recover you in the name of Jesus.

39. Every evil eye monitoring me for evil go blind, in the name of Jesus.

40. Pillars of success in my family shall not be pulled down in the name of Jesus.

41. Every grave spirit after my life, turn back from me and die in the name of Jesus.

42. Power assign to suck me like orange and throw me away, die in the name of Jesus.

43. I will not be a beggar or a moron in the name of Jesus.

44. My position shall not be dust bin of life, in the name of Jesus.

45. Every distraction against my dream, expire in the name of Jesus.

46. Any power, digging grave for me to be buried, enter the grave you dig, and be buried in it in the name of Jesus.

47. Coffin of darkness that has my wealth, break open and surrender my wealth to me, in the name of Jesus.

48. Every libation carried out against my destiny backfire and consume every power behind it, in the name of Jesus.

49. Satan, I challenge you to court of God, be detained forever, in the name of Jesus.

50. Every barrier erected against my life, break to pieces in the name of Jesus.

51. Magical power affecting me in the house I am now or in my previous house I slept or enter, expire, in the name of Jesus.

52. Every power that establish authority over me, expire with your authority in the name of Jesus.

53. I break the law of poverty over my life in the name of Jesus.

54. Every covenant of failure over my life, break in the name of Jesus.

55. O Lord, make me invisible and aggressive against powers of darkness in the name of Jesus.

56. Every excesses of darkness against my family, scatter and be nullified in the name of Jesus.

57. Breakthrough of God, flow into my life in the name of Jesus.

58. Powers assign to cripple my finance, expire in the name of Jesus.

59. Wind of darkness, blow against powers assigned to kill me in the name of Jesus.

60. It is war; my enemies shall surrender and die, in the name of Jesus.

61. It is war, let every stubborn pursuer, summersault and die in the name of Jesus.

CHAPTER 3

O LORD SILENCE THE VOW OF THE WICKED

Vows are statements that shouldn't be treated with clove's hand, either it is positive or negative vow. Positive vows are vows made to carry out good responsibility. These can be marriage vow, career vow, family vow of love, or saint committing oneself to an act, service or condition.

This chapter shall treat negative vow or vow of wickedness. Vow of wickedness is a vow made by enemy, witchcraft agents like herbalist, office co-workers, unfriendly friend, evil neighbor, satanic family member, church member, opposite religion member, to do evil against a person. Those who make such vow mean business. They mean to kill. They mean to bury your destiny. They mean to cause poverty in your life. They mean to cause sorrow and tears in your life. They mean to naked you. They consult evil places to settle scores with you. They mean to harm you, if possible, to make you run mad. They do everything possible to remove protection of God upon a life. They can fire arrow of prayerlessness into your life, so that you won't equip yourself with prayer or read Word of God.

It is catastrophic to be a victim of wicked vow. When vows are made, and given a follow up, victims fall into problems, even if you don't offend the person that made such vow. The fact is, a vow can be made against you and be innocent of it. Take for example, in a company where the personnel manager vowed he will not employ a particular tribe or race to occupy a particular office or position in the company; you are bound by the vow. This is more reason you must pray to cancel both known and unknown vow, both vow directed at you and one not directed at you.

Most times the wicked vow you will not make it. This is a direct vow against your personality, life and destiny. This is the vow that readily comes to mind when vow is mentioned. I pray, every vow directed at you shall fail in the name of Jesus. Witchcraft vow is dangerous; it limits life or cause outright death. Ladies that join witchcraft cult with vow to collect blood of victims or kill them or summon their souls for evil are destroyer of destiny. They hatch their plan with perfect hatred. Those that make wicked vow are dangerous, the vow they make is dangerous and they carry it out in a dangerous way. It is this dangerous mission that kills good vision; and when vision is polluted or destroyed, the destiny of victim runs southward. Such person may fall from great height, stumble or fall. It is pathetic to see victims of evil vow because they tell you story of how yester years are good. They tell you, they once live in duplex but now struggling to rent a room. As he talks, children are out of school. To feed is hectic, the clothe he wear is fade while his car is sold some years back. Things are not rosy anymore, because someone somewhere, carried out his/her evil vow against him. It now affects his destiny.

PRAYER POINTS

1. O Lord, I thank you, for silencing the vow of the wicked in the name of Jesus.

2. My father and my God, I thank you for your mercy upon me in the name of Jesus.

3. I thank my God, who makes way for me, where I conclude there is no way, in the name of Jesus.

4. O Lord, forgive me and make me great in the name of Jesus.

5. Lord Jesus, lay hand of forgiveness upon me in the name of Jesus.

6. O Lord, release me from generational sin in the name of Jesus.

7. Blood of Jesus, cleanse me of evil mark in the name of Jesus.

8. I cover myself with blood of Jesus against evil vow in the name of Jesus.

9. I drink blood of Jesus, to purify myself of evil deposit, in the name of Jesus.

10. Holy Ghost Fire, consume and destroy every wickedness that surround me in the name of Jesus.

11. O God arise fill me with Holy Ghost Fire, in the name of Jesus.

12. Holy Spirit, guide and guard me from evil arrow in the name of Jesus.

13. O Lord, give me strength to fulfill my vow in the house of God, in the name of Jesus.

14. O Lord, don't allow my vow work against me, in the name of Jesus.

15. O Lord my Father, accept my vow so that my life may move forward in the name of Jesus.

16. O Lord, let my vow overshadow the vow of the wicked in the name of Jesus.

17. Every vow of the wicked against me, scatter in the name of Jesus.

18. Every secret vow to pull me down, scatter, in the name of Jesus.

19. Witchcraft vow to silence me in my family, scatter in the name of Jesus.

20. Witchcraft vow that says I will bury my children, my life is not your candidate backfire and scatter, in the name of Jesus.

21. Witchcraft vow that says my career shall scatter, backfire in the name of Jesus.

22. Witchcraft vow that says I will graduate from one problem to another, backfire, in the name of Jesus.

23. Witchcraft vow aimed to bury my destiny scatter and backfire in the name of Jesus.

24. Oh heaven let the vow of the wicked work against them in the name of Jesus.

25. Every vow of the wicked working against me, backfire in the name of Jesus.

26. Every vow of the wicked making me to reap failure, stop by fire and expire in the name of Jesus.

27. Every vow of the wicked that created barriers around me, backfire in the name of Jesus.

28. Every barrier created as a result of evil vow, break, in the name of Jesus.

29. Dark vow against my credential scatter in the name of Jesus.

30. Oh heaven, let owner of evil vow, swallow venom of his vow and run mad in the name of Jesus.

31. Wicked vow of, "Thou shall not excel" spoken against my life, backfire in the name of Jesus.

32. Every vow made with idol of my father's house, scatter in the name of Jesus.

33. Dark agents that vow to carry out evil vow in my life, you are a liar, die in the name of Jesus.

34. Witch doctor, that vow his work against me shall prosper, you are not my God, die in the name of Jesus.

35. Every calendar and diary consulted at intervals for evil against me, catch fire and roast to ashes, in the name of Jesus.

36. Wicked vow to bury my talent scatter in the name of Jesus.

37. Every vow made with marine power to attack me, be reversed and favour me, in the name of Jesus.

38. Herbalist power against me, scatter in the name of Jesus.

39. Every dark vow against my marriage, scatter in the name of Jesus.

40. Every vow against my career and income, scatter in the name of Jesus.

41. Every worker in my place of work that vow to deal with me be put to shame in the name of Jesus.

42. Every unfriendly friend with evil intention against me, paralyze in the name of Jesus.

43. Unfriendly friend that work with enemies to harm me, be exposed and be disgraced in the name of Jesus.

44. Evil neighbor that vow to attack me, receive heavenly attack in the name of Jesus.

45. Powers holding my destiny captive; expire and rise no more in the name of Jesus.

46. My father and my God, silence every enemy that conspire to pull me down, in the name of Jesus.

47. Every dark padlock fashioned against my destiny, break to pieces, in the name of Jesus.

48. Any satanic person in my family that threaten to attack me, meet double failure, in the name of Jesus.

49. Any wicked member of my church that vow to deal with me, meet double failure in the name of Jesus.

50. Arrows of wicked vow from other religion against me backfire, in the name of Jesus.

51. Wicked forces that vow to kill me kill yourselves, in the name of Jesus.

52. Wicked forces that come together to attack me scatter, in the name of Jesus.

53. Every deadly tongue raging against me, backfire in the name of Jesus.

54. Every poisoned word pronounced against me, backfire in the name of Jesus.

55. Personalities within and around me, plotting evil against me, your time is up, die in the name of Jesus.

56. Any personality anywhere using charms to make me suffer, wherever you are, die in the name of Jesus.

57. Powers that vow to sink my destiny, you are a liar, die in the name of Jesus.

58. Powers that vow to shatter my dream die in the name of Jesus.

59. Every arrow of poverty fired against me backfire to the sender, in the name of Jesus.

60. Every arrow of stagnancy fired against my destiny backfire in the name of Jesus.

61. Every arrow of failure fired to scatter my destiny, backfire, in the name of Jesus.

62. Every arrow of bareness fired against my marriage backfire in the name of Jesus.

63. Every arrow of wickedness fired to turn my life upside down, backfire in the name of Jesus.

64. Every arrow of prayerlessness fired to stop my communication with God, backfire, in the name of Jesus.

65. Every witchcraft vow directed at me, backfire in the name of Jesus.

66. Every vow taken to collect my blood for evil, scatter in the name of Jesus.

67. Destroyers of destiny leave me alone and die, in the name of Jesus.

68. Every vow pronounced against me in the spirit to disgrace me, backfire in the name of Jesus.

69. Every dangerous mission embarked upon to destroy my destiny, scatter in the name of Jesus.

70. Every vow of darkness given follow up to destroy me, scatter in the name of Jesus.

71. I shall not fall victim of wicked vow, in the name of Jesus.

72. O Lord, let what I labored for manifest and bring me harvest in the name of Jesus.

73.O Lord, save me from evil doer in the name of Jesus.

CHAPTER 4

PRAYER TO KILL WITCHCRAFT SPIRIT WITHIN

Every Christian should take self-audit to know his spiritual status. You know yourself more than me, so is it with me. At least, I know my journey from age ten and above. I know my immediate family and a little, if not much of my extended or close family. I know the friends I keep and can tell little of their family. I know my school mates by name and attitude or habit of them that are close to me. All these are traces of people within your count. Though you may be young or old, you know yourself better than me.

The power that controls you is in you. That power resides in you. God deposits them in you, though there are some you develop in the course of upbringing, youth or old age. What God deposited in you is the godly gifts, the one you acquire contrary to God's righteousness is demonic gift. The evil one is called witchcraft spirit within.

Witchcraft spirit does not necessarily mean you are a witch, but your action can be equated as one. Witches are noted to kill, to steal and to destroy destiny, so are other spirits that are satanic. Witches and wizards, herbalists, marine spirits, occult spirits are often rejected as witchcraft spirit. But then, there are some spirits that either are planted in a life through witchcraft food or initiation, and or as a result of peer group. Spirit of drunkenness is a witchcraft spirit because it is an ungodly spirit that operates in a life. Spirit of lust is either inherited from parent gotten from peer group or developed inside of you as a result gullible mind, worldliness. Whichever way, witchcraft spirit is behind it all.

Witchcraft spirit influence different spirits to enter a life. There is spirit of stealing. Anyone with such spirit pick interest on whatever he sees with another person, or anything that do not belong to him. What will be in his mind is how to steal it and not be caught. There is spirit of murder. A person with this, think of death of his fellow man or woman. This is witchcraft spirit. Another spirit is, arson spirit. This is an non bail able offence, just like murder; since Satan is behind it, he wants you to die untimely death so that he may harvest your soul. He wants you to be frustrated and commit large scale offence and in order to nail you forever. The witchcraft power within you pushes you to do it.

When a person is controlled by these spirits, his destiny is at stake. He needs to prepare for war. He should know there is war. He has to take his matter to the Almighty God the killer of evil powers and father of righteousness. What is not righteous is ungodly, and what is ungodly is evil. So when you take your matter to God, with repentance, God will arise and help you out. That spirit, assign to eliminate you shall be eliminated.

Brethren, it is time for war! Rise up like soldier of Christ, immunize and be loaded with blood of Jesus to withstand pressure from Satan. Crown yourself with fire of victory, equip yourself with weapon of warfare, cry for anointing from the heavenly to conquer and march forward against powers and principalities that plant evil in the life of people. That witchcraft spirit that lives in you must come out today. Every unforgiving spirit must die. The Lord shall exterminate all and you shall be made whole today in the name of Jesus. Amen.

PRAYER POINTS

1. I thank you Lord for your protection upon my life, in the name of Jesus.

2. I thank God that makes me witness this day in the name of Jesus.

3. I thank my God who made it possible for me to discover myself in the name of Jesus.

4. O Lord, forgive me so that I may grow in your Word in the name of Jesus.

5. Oh heaven open, let rains of forgiveness fall upon me, in the name of Jesus.

6. Lord Jesus, lay hands of forgiveness upon me in the name of Jesus.

7. I drink blood of Jesus to purge me of evil deposit in the name of Jesus.

8. I cover myself with blood of Jesus to reverse evil arrow fired against me, in the name of Jesus.

9. Blood of Jesus, flow around me, in the name of Jesus.

10. Holy Spirit, hold me to you in the name of Jesus.

11. Holy Ghost Fire, burn every witchcraft attachment around me in the name of Jesus.

12. Holy Ghost Power, dwell in my life, in the name of Jesus.

13. O Lord, baptize me with spirit of righteousness in the name of Jesus.

14. O Lord, set my journey straight, in the name of Jesus.

15. O Lord, safe me from family captivity of idolatry in the name of Jesus.

16. O Lord, let every contrary spirit in me, come out and die, in the name of Jesus.

17. Every contrary spirit speaking evil against me die, in the name of Jesus.

18. Spirit of lust, living in my body come out and die, in the name of Jesus.

19. Spirit of murder, ruling in my spirit, get out of me in the name of Jesus.

20. Spirit of stealing, assign to cause me shame, leave my soul, in the name of Jesus.

21. Spirit of arson, dwelling in my life to manifest later, die in the name of Jesus.

22. Sprit of failure inhabited in my life, come out and die in the name of Jesus.

23. Spirit of prayerlessness shall not take over my life die in the name of Jesus.

24. Spirit of loneliness, my life is not your candidate die in the name of Jesus.

25. Spirit of procrastination, quit my life stop disturbing me, in the name of Jesus.

26. Spirit of hatred in my life, that distanced me from helpers, die in the name of Jesus.

27. Spirit of mockery, quit my life, let me face path of breakthrough in the name of Jesus.

28. Spirit of idolatry, troubling my destiny catch fire and roast to ashes, in the name of Jesus.

29. Spirit of witchcraft shall not kill me in the name of Jesus.

30. Spirit of uncleanness assign to pollute me, die in the name of Jesus.

31. Every attack from my immediate family, scatter in the name of Jesus.

32. Every arrow fired against me when I was young, come out of me, backfire to your sender in the name of Jesus.

33. Every arrow fired from friends when I was young, backfire in the name of Jesus.

34. Every witchcraft food I ate in the dream, I vomit you, in the name of Jesus.

35. Every witchcraft food I cannot vomit in the dream, dry up in the name of Jesus.

36. Every witchcraft food that refuse to dry up, be neutralized and be useless in the name of Jesus.

37. Spirit of drunkenness enemy introduced to my life, come out of me and die, in the name of Jesus.

38. Every evil counsel assign to captivate my soul, scatter and backfire in the name of Jesus.

39. O Lord, let rage of the enemy against me scatter, in the name of Jesus.

40. Powers seeking my head on the platter of darkness, I cut your neck with sword of God, in the name of Jesus.

41. O Lord, break the teeth of the ungodly that vow to destroy me in the name of Jesus.

42. Occult spirit world I am initiated with, I break myself loose from it in the name of Jesus.

43. Marine spirit controlling my spirit, I break myself loose from you, in the name of Jesus.

44. Marine spirit; summoning my spirit for initiation die in the name of Jesus.

45. Witchcraft power assign to kill good things in my life, die in the name of Jesus.

46. Witchcraft power assign to poison me, my life is not your candidate die in the name of Jesus.

47. Witchcraft power from outside that join hands with witches in my family to destroy me, die in the name of Jesus.

48. Witchcraft spirit living in me I suffocate you with power in the blood of Jesus in the name of Jesus.

49. Every negative plants in my life assign to control me, wither and die, in the name of Jesus.

50. Let fire fall and consume powers that vow I will be mincemeat in their witchcraft kitchen in the name of Jesus.

51. Power that vow to drag me on the floor, die in the name of Jesus.

52. Witchcraft power assign to steal from me, your time is up, die in the name of Jesus.

53. Witches and wizards that implant dark spirit in me, carry your evil load, in the name of Jesus.

54. Enemies of my family, receive double disgrace in the name of Jesus.

55. O Lord, pull me out of every hidden net of the enemy in the name of Jesus.

56. O Lord, let the wicked against my soul be ashamed, let them die and be silent in the grave in the name of Jesus.

57. O Lord, reveal to me deep secret I need to know about my lineage, so that I may move forward in life, in the name of Jesus.

58. Every arrow of nakedness fired against me backfire in the name of Jesus.

59. Satanic altar in high places in my father's house, catch fire and roast to ashes in the name of Jesus.

60. Every covenant with dark powers break in the name of Jesus.

61. Every evil voice speaking against my sanity, backfire in the name of Jesus.

62. Let the sun and the moon arise, and fight every diviner assign against me, in the name of Jesus.

63. Whatever enemy programmed into my life, I deprogram you in the name of Jesus.

64. Every demonic operation carried out in the night against my soul, scatter in the name of Jesus.

65. Witchcraft power using the sand to control my soul, die in the name of Jesus.

66. Every incantation against my soul backfire in the name of Jesus.

67. Every sacrifice of darkness aimed to scatter my plan and make me poor, scatter in the name of Jesus.

68.Every environmental altar monitoring my life, catch fire and roast to ashes, in the name of Jesus.

69.O Lord, reveal secrets behind my problem in the name of Jesus.

70.I receive power to disgrace my enemy in the name of Jesus.

71.I bind and rebuke dark Princes ad powder controlling my soul in the name of Jesus.

72.I break all agreement I made with dark powers in the name of Jesus.

73.Evil mouth that vomit evil food to my mouth while I was a baby, paralyze in the name of Jesus.

74.Every bewitchment in my life, expire in the name of Jesus.

75.Holy Angel, carry warfare back to the owner in the name of Jesus.

76.Every activity of witchcraft in my family, I paralyze you, in the name of Jesus.

77. Agenda of darkness for my life, scatter in the name of Jesus.

78. Every dark cloud over my habitation, clear away in the name of Jesus.

79. Every band of wickedness around me, scatter in the name of Jesus.

80. In this battle, I shall win and not lose, in the name of Jesus.

81. I dedicate my life to God, in the name of Jesus.

82. O Lord, deliver my soul to Christ in the name of Jesus.

CHAPTER 5

I ARISE AND KILL STUBBORN PURUSERS THAT WILL NOT LET ME GO

Stubborn pursuers, as the name connotes are stubborn witchcraft agents that will never let you go. They don't leave their victim alone until they carry out their evil. They harass and mortgage life. They are boastful and wicked. They are selfish and arrogant. They think most for themselves. They have little regard for others. Stubborn pursuers see something in you before he pick on you. It may be your talent, your star, wealth, wisdom, joy, favor of God upon you etc. stubborn pursuers are dedicated for a purpose; to ruin a life. They demote and devalue life. They don't put smiles in the face of people.

From the above you can see that they are not the type of people you shake hands with. If someone is promoted in office and against you, he is a stubborn pursuer that targets career of others. He doesn't want food on your table. He hates your cup full. Stubborn pursuers hate you to hold cup of wine or fruit juice in the hand. He hates you laugh. He wants you to be in agony, sorrow and regret. Stubborn pursuer is a master at evil. If you lose your job, or you are sacked your dignity at home reduces, respect accorded you is gone to the wind. Such a situation gives neighbors opportunity to laugh at you. They ask strange questions like:- What is the problem with him? Does he steal? Is he incompetent in office? Did he steal in office? Is there downsize in his office? What may have caused it? So they will ask. They ask all these, to know how they will react at you or make fun of you. Brethren, unemployment is bad. It makes one redundant and look stupid at times. "There is nothing in his upstairs", some people will say. If you know a stubborn pursuer that wants to put you in this condition, what will you do? I know you will say, "God forbid". Yes, God forbid, it is not your portion, but then you must rise up and kill every spirit and forces that may rise up to destroy your destiny, your future and your peace.

Look at the life of the children of Israel. They were in bondage for many years after the death of Pharaoh that knew them. They enjoyed and danced years back before a new Pharaoh was enthroned. It is not that the new Pharaoh didn't know the history of his country of how Joseph saved their grandparents from starvation, but different spirit took over hm. He converted the children of Israel to servant or at best slaves. This is the condition they found themselves until one day, they remembered there is One God called Yahweh. They cried to Yahweh, and he answered them. I pray, your cry and prayer to Yahweh against stubborn pursuers shall be answered today, in the name of Jesus. Amen

After much resistance to Moses demand to Pharaoh to release children of Israel to worship God in the wilderness, he let them go. But not after he lost his first born son, as it was to every home in Egypt. Every home lost their first born son. There was outcry in the land, but no one die in the house of Israel. Pharaoh surrendered and let them go. No sooner they left, he changed his mind, he wants the slaves back. He ordered his able bodied men to mount on horse to pursue and bring them back. They did, but in the course lost out. I pray, every stubborn pursuer after you shall fail in your life in the name of Jesus. They pursued the children of Israel, even to the Red Sea. When they saw the children of Israel passed through dry ground in such mighty Sea, they followed suit. They lost their senses of what God did to their first born not quite long. What happened now is, they all perished in the Red Sea when they entered it to capture the Israelites. Here, I decree into your life, every stubborn pursuer that refuse to let you go shall perish in the Red Sea, in the order of Egyptians.

Brethren, you can now see, God is a killer. Invite Him to your situation now and kill every stubborn pursuer that rise up against you. It is time you go into spiritual warfare to kill and destroy every stubborn pursuer that will not let you go.

PRAYER POINTS

1. O Lord, I thank you for your power that delivered me from every bondage in the name of Jesus.

2. I thank you Lord, for your unrelenting affection for me, in the name of Jesus.

3. I thank you Lord for your mercy and love for me, in the name of Jesus.

4. O Lord, have mercy on me and forgive me, in the name of Jesus.

5. Lord Jesus, let today be my day of visitation and forgiveness, blot my sins out of book of sinners in the name of Jesus.

6. Evil yoke of sin in my life; break in the name of Jesus.

7. I receive the covering of blood of Jesus against witchcraft arrow in the name of Jesus.

8. By the power in the blood of Jesus, I break every blood covenant I have with witchcraft power in the name of Jesus.

9. I soak my blood, bones and flesh in the blood of Jesus, and I am set free in the name of Jesus.

10. Blood of Jesus, laminate my life in the name of Jesus.

11. Holy Ghost Fire, anoint my tongue in the name of Jesus.

12. Holy Spirit, reveal deep secret of stubborn pursuer to me in the name of Jesus.

13. Every satanic retaliation against me backfire in the name of Jesus.

14. Every marine altar set up to afflict me, catch fire and roast to ashes, in the name of Jesus.

15. Wicked invasion of the enemy against me scatter in the name of Jesus.

16. I silence the voice of stubborn pursuers after my life, in the name of Jesus.

17. O God arise, deliver me from the hands of stubborn pursuer in the name of Jesus.

18. Every stubborn witchcraft agent after my life, die in the name of Jesus.

19. Powers that vow, he will not let me go, my life is not your candidate, expire in the name of Jesus.

20. Powers assign to harass and mortgage my life, your time is up, expire in the name of Jesus.

21. Thou wicked boastful power after my life, paralyze in the name of Jesus.

22. Spirit of selfishness that stare enemies to attack me, work against yourself in the name of Jesus.

23. You arrogant power pursuing me day and night, expire in the name of Jesus.

24. Powers assign to attack my talent so that I may be poor, my life is not your candidate, expire in the name of Jesus.

25. Powers assigned to attack my star, you are a failure, expire in the name of Jesus.

26. Power assigned to attack my wealth, enough is enough, expire and rise no more, in the name of Jesus.

27. Powers assign to pollute my wisdom, fail in your mission in the name of Jesus.

28. Stubborn pursuers that want me and my family to drink from cup of sorrow, meet double failure, in the name of Jesus.

29. Powers that want sorrow to replace laughter in my mouth, shall fail in the name of Jesus.

30. My foundation, receive heavenly deliverance in the name of Jesus.

31. Stubborn pursuers after my life; lose your sense and run mad in the name of Jesus.

32. Stubborn pursuers dedicated against me in office, meet double failure in the name of Jesus.

33. Every prison yard I am kept in the spirit by evil power, break open, I march to freedom in the name of Jesus.

34. Holy Ghost Fire, pursue my pursuer in the name of Jesus.

35. Owner of evil load carry your load in the name of Jesus.

36. Storm of confusion; possess the camp of my enemy in the name of Jesus.

37. Any personality assign to sabotage my progress, run mad in the name of Jesus.

38. Foundational bondage, troubling my soul; scatter in the name of Jesus.

39. Fire of God, make me whole; consume every work of darkness in the name of Jesus.

40. Anointing of success, my life is available, come upon me in the name of Jesus.

41. Messenger of death, turn back with your message and die in the name of Jesus.

42. Seed of poverty planted in my family wither and die in the name of Jesus.

43. Any power hired to curse my destiny, die in the name of Jesus.

44. Every enchantment and sorcery against my destiny backfire in the name of Jesus.

45. Every witchcraft challenge against my life, scatter in the name of Jesus.

46. Every terror of the night against my destiny scatter in the name of Jesus.

47. O God arise, let stubborn problem in my life expire, in the name of Jesus.

48. Witchcraft vulture waiting for my flesh, die in the name of Jesus.

49. Every power of my father's house that vow I will not make it in life, expire in the name of Jesus.

50. Any power that will not let me go, when my God says go, your time is up die, in the name of Jesus.

51. Every bitter river flowing into my life, dry up in the name of Jesus.

52. Yoke of stagnancy in my life, break in the name of Jesus.

53. Strange prophecy against my life, backfire in the name of Jesus.

54. O Lord, mobilize the resources of heaven and favour me in the name of Jesus.

55. Power assigned to ruin my life shall fail die in the name of Jesus.

56. Stubborn pursuers after my health, your time is up, die in the name of Jesus.

57. Every arrow of darkness fired by stubborn pursuers against my life, backfire in the name of Jesus.

58. Every arrow of slow death fired against my life; backfire in the name of Jesus.

59. Every arrow of sorrow fired against my life; backfire in the name of Jesus.

60. Every arrow of bareness fired against my destiny; backfire in the name of Jesus.

61. Every arrow of poverty fired against my life; backfire in the name of Jesus.

62. Every arrow of the valley fired against my life, backfire in the name of Jesus.

63. Every strongman dedicated against my destiny, die in the name of Jesus.

64. Every adversary after my destiny, scatter in the name of Jesus.

65. Witchcraft chain assign for me in the spirit, break to pieces in the name of Jesus.

66. Every enemy of my breakthrough, die in the name of Jesus.

67. Every weapon of shame dedicated against my life, in order to frustrate me, catch fire and roast to ashes, in the name of Jesus.

68. Woe to every troubler of Israel of my life, in the name of Jesus.

69. Every captivity fashioned against me in the spirit, scatter in the name of Jesus.

70. Every activity of stubborn pursuers against my life, scatter in the name of Jesus.

71. Every power hindering my breakthrough die in the name of Jesus.

72. Witchcraft bondage, limiting my laughter, scatter in the name of Jesus.

73.Deliverance anger of God, work against stubborn pursuers after my life in the name of Jesus.

74.Every altar of darkness, speaking hardship to my life, catch fire and roast to ashes, in the name of Jesus.

75.O Lord, let frustration in my life reverse and be point of breakthrough turn around in my life, in the name of Jesus.

76.Power of liberty and dignity manifest in my life in the name of Jesus.

77.I shall arise; no power shall pull me down in the name of Jesus.

78.My enemy shall bow and lick the dust in the name of Jesus.

79.Fire of God, separate me from power of darkness, in the name of Jesus.

80.Encircle me O Lord, with wall of fire, in the name of Jesus.

81.Enemy shall not bury my talent in the name of Jesus.

82. Favor of God, my life is available enter in the name of Jesus.

83. Light of God, shine upon me in the name of Jesus.

84. O Lord, increase my vision and glory against the wish of the enemy, in the name of Jesus.

85. O Lord my God, let me be exalted to glorify your name in the name of Jesus.

CHAPTER 6

PRAYER WHEN IN ANGUISH

Prayer when in anguish is a situation of soberness. A person in anguish is bitter at heart. He wants things done but with little likelihood of clarity success. Power and ability to do it may be there, but is handicapped at this material time. He needs to summon courage to face the situation. Someone in anguish may lose focus if distraction is much. The mind of an anguish person is unsettled, he hardly concentrates. Anguish at times lead to loneliness when you can hardly be pacified. Anguish can make one think negative.

When the children of Israel were in anguish under King Xerxes, Haman plotted to kill the Jews. It brought fear to their mind. Haman was given a seat of honor higher than that of all other nobles. The cause of the anguish is, *"All the royal officials at the kings gate kneel down and paid honor to Haman, for the king had commanded this concerning him. But Mordecai could not kneel down or pay him honor". Esther 3:2* This act annoyed Haman, for this reason he planned to eliminate all the Jews. A law was passed by the king through Haman's instigation; this made all Jews in the land unhappy. They were in anguish all this while, until Queen Esther was contacted.

She gave word of advice to the Jews to fast for three days. *"Go gather together all the Jews who are in Susa, and fast for me, do not eat and drink for three night and day. I and my maids will fast as you do. When this is done, I will go to the King, even though it is against the law. And if I perish, I perish." Esther 4:16.* Queen Esther took drastic step to end the drastic action of Haman.

After the three days dry fast, Queen Esther went before the King. Along the line Mordecai was honored more than Haman after the book of Chronicles was read by the king. This angered Haman and he went and hanged himself in the gallows he built for Mordecai. I pray, any evil planned for you by the enemy, he will be the person that will be consumed by it. If Mordecai had not taken step to meet Queen Esther, anguish and sudden death would have been their portion. The lesson is, in time of anguish look for solution. Never give up. The God that have license to kill shall arise and put everything in shape. At this point, I prophesy into your life, no anguish shall consume you or anyone in your family. Amen.

Nehemiah was in anguish when he got report of situations about the remnants of Israel who survived the exile and were back at home. He learnt they were in great trouble and disgrace. The wall of Jerusalem is broken down, and its gates have been burned with fire. This is what enemies want for you and your family. They want you to be in sorrow and in disgrace. They want you to be in great shock, live in penury and beg for food. But I know, by the power of the Living God, all these shall not be your portion.

Anguish is not a license to alienate you from answer. It is an opportunity for you to grow. You don't need to look back or be stagnant. Doors and windows of opportunities are open, only if you can recognize it. Anguish doesn't mean you stand along or be tired of life. You must find solution rather than complain. In the case of Nehemiah, he seeks the face of God when it matters most. Hear him, ***"When I heard these things, I sat down and wept. For some days I mourned and wept. For some days I mourned and fasted and pray before the God of heaven" Nehemiah 1:4.***

Nehemiah took his request and matter to God in petition and in prayer. God gave him strength and wisdom to talk to the king for permission to rebuild the wall of Jerusalem. Despite opposition from enemies, Nehemiah built the wall. If Nehemiah did not take action, the wall wouldn't have been built. The threat of attack against the builder did not deter him. He completed the work and earn a landmark remark.

Brethren, whatever you may lose before now, whatever enemies destroy in your life, whatever needs repair in you, God shall rise and do it. You should not lose hope or surrender, pray for grace and favour in the manner of Nehemiah who seek God's favour and mercy before going to the king who as well favoured him with mercy. I pray, you shall see favour of God and of man wherever you go. The Lord that has license to kill shall kill the moral of your enemies. They shall experience double portion of disgrace in the name of Jesus.

Job was in anguish when he lost all to the wind. He lost his properties and children within a twinkling of an eye. Job lost everything and was in anguish, but he never insulted God or question Him, by saying, "Why me God?" Rather he fell on the ground and worshiped him. It is not easy to compose self if such calamity before one. Later, he showed anguish in his speech when his three friends visited him to sympathize with him. This is when Satan afflicted him with sores. How will you feel if pains are all over your body? The pains made Job to curse the day he was born.

Anguish is not a good thing; you must pray to live above it. Anguish makes you look sober and worrisome. Today is the day, the Lord with license to kill, shall arise and silence every power behind challenges and problem in your life. The Lord shall arise and bury your problem. The Lord shall arise and favor you. The Lord shall arise and have mercy upon you. The Lord shall arise and enlarge your coast. The Lord shall arise and put smiles in your face, in the name of Jesus.

PRAYER POINTS

1. I thank you Lord, for removing anguish in my life, in the name of Jesus.

2. I thank my God, who shall put smiles to my face in the name of Jesus.

3. I thank my God, who blesses me in every way I turn, in the name of Jesus.

4. O Lord, let your grace and favor be my portion in the name of Jesus.

5. O Lord, forgive me every sin in my life, in the name of Jesus.

6. Lord Jesus, let mercy and forgiveness be my portion, in the name of Jesus.

7. Blood of Jesus, heal every wound in my body, in the name of Jesus.

8. Blood of Jesus, cleanse every mark of defeat in my body in the name of Jesus.

9. I drink blood of Jesus, to purge me of any impurity in my body in the name of Jesus.

10. Holy Spirit, dwell in me in the name of Jesus.

11. Holy Ghost Fire, burn to ashes any attachment of darkness in my life, in the name of Jesus.

12. Angels of God, cover me with feather of God and minister to me in the name of Jesus.

13. Every situation of sadness in my life, expire in the name of Jesus.

14. Every bitterness in my heart, expire, in the name of Jesus.

15. O Lord, give me clarity of success in whatever I do, in the name of Jesus.

16. O Lord, give me courage to face every situation and bring it to normal in the name of Jesus.

17. I shall not lose focus or be distracted in the journey of life, in the name of Jesus.

18. Every spirit of loneliness dwelling in me, come out and expire in the name of Jesus.

19. Every plot of the enemy to kill me, scatter and backfire, in the name of Jesus.

20. O Lord, give me seat of honour in my father's house, in the name of Jesus.

21. Every fear of the unknown troubling my soul, expire and be useless, in the name of Jesus.

22. Satanic commandment to kneel down and bow before my enemy, shall fail in the name of Jesus.

23.Every set date and hour enemy plan to eliminate me shall fail in the name of Jesus.

24.Every negative thought as a result of anguish, expire, in the name of Jesus.

25.Every instigation against me scatter in the name of Jesus.

26.Every food of sorrow prepared for me in the spirit, catch fire and roast to ashes, in the name of Jesus.

27.Every garment of sorrow sown for me in the spirit, I tear you to pieces and set it ablaze in the name of Jesus.

28.Powers that gathered against my success; scatter in the name of Jesus.

29.Powers that gathered together against my success; scatter in the name of Jesus.

30.Any spirit that says, I will perish, shall replace me, and perish in the name of Jesus.

31.The gallows enemies built for me; shall kill them in the name of Jesus.

32. Gallows of darkness in my dream; expire in the name of Jesus.

33. Every evil, enemy planned for me scatter, in the name of Jesus.

34. Every arrow of sudden death fired against me; backfire in the name of Jesus.

35. O Lord, that have license to kill, scatter and destroy forces of darkness after my life, in the name of Jesus.

36. Any power assign to put my family in ruin, die, in the name of Jesus.

37. Any power boasting my house shall be remnant, you are not my God die in the name of Jesus.

38. I shall not be in exile, in the name of Jesus.

39. Those who boast I shall die in great trouble shall fail, in the name of Jesus.

40. Satan shall not expose my life to insecurity around me in the name of Jesus.

41. As the mountains surround Jerusalem, so shall the Lord surrounds me with heavenly angels, in the name of Jesus.

42. O Lord, break every chain of darkness assign for me, in the name of Jesus.

43. For my sake, O Lord rebuke Kings in the name of Jesus.

44. Powers that vow I will eat ashes as food, O Lord make them eat ashes as food, in the name of Jesus.

45. Every river of sadness flowing to my life, dry up in the name of Jesus.

46. Forces that join together against me, let earth open and swallow them in the name of Jesus.

47. Angels of God, destroy my enemies for the wickedness meted on me in the name of Jesus.

48. Powers delaying me to dwell in the shelter of the Most High shall fail in the name of Jesus.

49. Every deadly power hunting my life, die in the name of Jesus.

50. Every strange shock planned for me, scatter in the name of Jesus.

51. Powers and personalities that boast I will come to them to beg for food shall fail and die with their boast in the name of Jesus.

52. I shall not live in penury in the name of Jesus.

53. Every terror of the night against me, expire in the name of Jesus.

54. Every power that vow I will not rest in the shadow of the Almighty shall die and rise no more in the name of Jesus.

55. O Lord, give me strength and wisdom to perfect my life, in the name of Jesus.

56. Powers waiting for the day I will cry, I am not your candidate die, in the name of Jesus.

57. O Lord, I take permission and authority to re-build what is down in my family, in the name of Jesus.

58. Whatever I lost in the past, I recover them all in the name of Jesus.

59. Whatever is destroyed in my life, resurrect by the power in the blood of Jesus.

60. Whatever needs repair in my life, O Lord repair it in the name of Jesus.

61. Heavenly landmark reward my life is available enter in the name of Jesus.

62. Every arrow of calamity fired against me backfire, in the name of Jesus.

63. Every affliction troubling my soul, expire in the name of Jesus.

64. Stubborn pursuers after my life, receive double portion of disgrace in the name of Jesus.

65. I shall not bow down to enemies in the name of Jesus.

66. O Lord, connect me to helpers at time of need, in the name of Jesus.

67. Every arrow of disgrace fired against me backfire in the name of Jesus.

68. Powers assigned to burn down my house in the spirit die in the name of Jesus.

69. Weeping and sorrow shall not be my portion in the name of Jesus.

70. I will not mourn in the name of Jesus.

71. Every plague assign to consume me, consume your owner in the name of Jesus.

72. Every fowler snare dedicated to captivate me in the spirit, catch fire and roast to ashes, in the name of Jesus.

73. O Lord, give me power to trample upon lion and serpent unhurt in the name of Jesus.

74. With long life, I shall dwell on this earth with peace in the name of Jesus.

75. O Lord, silence all the wicked that rise up to destroy my destiny in the name of Jesus.

76. O Lord, curse those who cursed me in the name of Jesus.

77. Every cloud of darkness around me, scatter, in the name of Jesus.

78. Spirit to fast and pray to seek face of God and get what I need, come upon me in the name of Jesus.

79. O Lord; show me the path to take, in the name of Jesus.

80. I prophesy to my life and family, anguish shall not scatter my plan in the name of Jesus.

81. I prophesy to my life, no anguish shall consume me, in the name of Jesus.

82. Every covenant of God for my life, come alive in the name of Jesus.

83. As far as the heavens are above the earth, so shall problem will be far from me in the name of Jesus.

84. As far as the heavens are above the earth so shall sorrow be far from me, in the name of Jesus.

85. As far as the east is from the west, so far shall anguish be far from me, in the name of Jesus.

86. As far as the east is from the west, so far shall poverty be far from me, in the name of Jesus.

87. By the power of the Living God, I shall not lose anything to the wind, in the name of Jesus.

88. By the power of the Living God, soberness and worries shall not locate me in the name of Jesus.

89. By the power of the Living God, my God shall arise and bury my problem in the name of Jesus.

90. By the power of the Living God, my God shall arise and enlarge my coast, in the name of Jesus.

91. By the power of the Living God, my God shall arise and put smiles in my face, in the name of Jesus.

YOU HAVE BATTLES TO WIN
TRY THESE BOOKS

1. COMMAND THE DAY: DAILY PRAYER BOOK

Each day of the week is loaded with meanings and divine assurance. God did not create each day of the week for the fun of it. Blessings, success, gifts, resources, hopes, portfolios, duties, rights, prophecies, warnings and challenges, are loaded in each day.

Do you know the language, command or decree you can use to claim what belongs to you in each day of the week? Do you know in Christendom, Monday can be equated to one of the days of creation in Genesis chapter one? Do you know creation lasted for six days and God rested on the seventh day? What day of the week can Christian equate as the first day of the week, if we follow Christian calendar? What day can we call day seven?

This book shall give insight to these questions. It shall explain how you can command each day of the week according to creation in the book of Genesis chapter one.

Above all, you shall exercise your right and claim what is hidden in each day of the week.
Check for this in **COMMAND THE DAY: DAILY PRAYER BOOK**

2. PRAYER TO REMEMBER DREAMS

A lot of people are passing through this spiritual epidemic on a daily basis. Their dream life is epileptic, having no ability to remember all dreams they dream, or sometimes forget everything entirely. This is nothing but spiritual havoc you need to erase from your spiritual record.
The answer to every form of spiritual blackout caused by spiritual erasers is found in, **PRAYER TO REMEMBER DREAMS**

3. 100% CONFESSIONS AND PROPHECIES TO LOCATE HELPERS AND HELPERS TO LOCATE YOU

This is a wonderful book on confessions and prophecies to locate helpers and helpers to locate you. It is a prayer book loaded with over two thousand (2,000) prayer points.

The book unravels how to locate unknown helpers, prayers to arrest mind of helpers and prayers for manifestation after encounter with helpers.

4. <u>ANOINTING FOR ELEVENTH HOUR HELP: HOPE AND HELP FOR YOUR TURBULENT TIMES</u>

This book tells much of what to do at injury hour called eleventh hour. When you read and use this book as prescribed fear shall vanish in your life when pursuing a project, career or contract.

5. <u>PRAYER TO LOCATE HELPERS AND HELPERS TO LOCATE YOU</u>

Our divine helper is God. He created us to be together and be of help to one another. In the midst of no help we lost out, ending our journey in the wilderness.

There are keys assign to open right doors of life. You need right key to locate your helpers. Enough is enough; of suffering in silence.

With this book, you shall locate your helpers while your helpers shall locate you.

6. <u>FIRE FOR FIRE PART ONE: (PRAYER BOOK BOOK 1)</u>

This prayer book is fast at answering spiritual problems. It is a bulldozer prayer book, full of prayers all through. It is highly recommended for night vigil. Testimonies are pouring in daily from users of this book across the world!

7. <u>PRAYER FOR FRUIT OF THE WOMB: EXPECTING MOTHERS</u>

This prayer book is children magnet. By faith and believe in God Almighty, as soon as you use this book open doors to child bearing shall be yours. Amen

8. <u>PRAYER FOR PREGNANT WOMEN: WITH ALL CHRISTIAN NAMES AND MEANINGS</u>

This is a spiritual prayer book loaded with prayers of solution for pregnant women. As soon as you take in, the prayers you shall pray from day one of conception to the day of delivery are written in this book.

9. <u>**WARFARE IN THE OFFICE: PRAYER TO SILENCE TOUGH TIMES IN OFFICE**</u>

It is high time you pray prayers of power must change hands in office. Use this book and liberate yourself from every form of office yoke.

10. <u>**MY MARRIAGE SHALL NOT BREAK: THE SECRET TO LOVE AND MARRIAGE THAT LASTS**</u>

Marriage is corner piece of life, happiness and joy. You need to hold it tight and guide it from wicked intruders and destroyer of homes.

11. <u>**VICTORY OVER SATANIC HOUSE PART ONE: RIDDING YOUR HOME OF SPIRITUAL DARKNESS**</u>

Are you a tenant, Land lord bombarded left and right, front and back by wicked people around you?
With this book you shall be liberated from the hooks of the enemy.

12. <u>**DICTIONARY OF DREAMS: THE DREAM INTERPRETATION**</u>

DICTIONARY WITH SYMBOLS, SIGNS, AND MEANINGS

This is a must book for every home. It gives accurate details to about **10,000 (Ten thousand) dreams and interpretations,** written in alphabetical order for quick reference and easy digestion. The book portrays spiritual revelations with sound prophetic guidelines. It is loaded with Biblical references and violent prayers.
Ask for yours today.

For Further Enquiries Contact
**THE AUTHOR
EVANGELIST TELLA OLAYERI
P.O. Box 1872 Shomolu Lagos.
Tel: 08023583168**

FROM AUTHOR'S DESK

BEFORE YOU GO

Hello,

Thank you for purchasing this book. Would you consider posting a review about this book? In addition to providing feedback and arousing others into Christ's bosom, reviews can help other customers to know about the book.

Please take a minute to leave a review on this book.

I would appreciate that!

Thank you in advance, for your review and your patronage!!

Feel free to drop us your prayer request. We will join faith with you and God's power will be released in your life and issue in question.

http://tellaolayeri.com/prayerrequest.php

NOTE: You can get all my books from my website http://tellaolayeri.com

GOOD NEWS!!!

My audiobook is now available, to get one visit **acx.com** and search **"Tella Olayeri."**

Brethren, to be loaded and reloaded visit: amazon.com/author/tellaolayeri for a full spiritual sojourn for my books.

Thanks.

9 798671 985658